Discovering the miraculous in the mundane

by Kristen Cottingham

Life Beyond Laundry

ISBN: 978-0-9792739-7-1
Printed in the United States of America
©2008 by Kristen Cottingham
All rights reserved

Cover and interior design by Isaac Publishing, Inc.

Library of Congress Number: 2008934829

Isaac Publishing, Inc.
P.O. 342
Three Rivers, MI 49093
www.isaacpublishing.com

No part of this book may be reproduced or transmitted in any form
or by any means, electronic or mechanical—including photocopying,
recording, or by any information storage and retrieval system—
without permission in writing from the publisher, except as provided
by United States of America copyright law.

Please direct your inquiries to admin@isaacpublishing.com

This book is dedicated to my children,
Carley, Alex, Cameron and Madison.
I love you so much that I can only *imagine* how deep
God's love must be!
And to my husband, Chad,
your unconditional love and steadfast belief in me
exemplifies God's faithfulness –
I love you!

With special thanks to
my mother, Judy Dense', for her strength and godly
example which laid a firm foundation of faith in my life
and my mother-in-law, Marian Cottingham, whose
sacrificial love and generosity toward her family is a
tremendous blessing.

And in honor of
Jim Dense' and Gary Cottingham
whose memory lives in my heart.

You are all proof that God is real!

LIFE BEYOND LAUNDRY

Discovering the miraculous in the mundane

Life beyond laundry – is there such a thing? Is there really more to life than the overflowing clothes hamper sitting outside my bedroom door?

As a mother of four children, sometimes I feel there is no end in sight to the mundane chore of laundry. Just when I think I'm finished, wham! Something else gets thrown in. Keeping up with the never-ending piles of clothes is a constant battle. And unlike my bulging laundry basket, this task leaves my heart feeling empty. Too often I ask myself, "Is this normal?" I long to be defined by something more than daily chores – more than successfully sorting whites from colors!

If only we would poke our head out of the dryer long enough, we would hear God's voice softly beckon. His gentle whisper suggests we are crafted for something more than simply waiting for the dryer buzzer to sound. He longs to clean the lint off our "filters" and invites us to discover a world far beyond our mundane routines.

By taking a step back from the spin cycle of life, we are able to see God is there – waiting to pour His miraculous wonders right into the middle of our mundane! God wants us to know Him as He reveals Himself through the world around us. Life takes on new meaning, as we understand God's purpose goes beyond our circumstances. We also discover He is completely able to Wash out our sins, Rinse away our hurt, Dry our tears, Carry our load, Iron out life's wrinkles, Refresh our spirit and Spin us in a new direction!

By unfolding my personal experiences of discovering miraculous in the mundane, my hope is that you will begin to view your everyday cycle differently. I pray you will look at life from a new perspective – one that is attentive to the miraculous all around!

The "Sort it Out" section following each story is intended for your personal application. These thoughts are designed to pull your heart toward God, bring encouragement and spark the beginning of an exciting journey - one that goes so far beyond - that "normal" turns out to be just a setting on your washing machine!

A GOOD GIFT

My husband, Chad, and I decided to take advantage of a recent snowfall and hit the snowmobile trails. Early one morning we loaded up the trailer and made a two-hour trip north. Anticipation grew as the fresh white fluff called out as clear as the blue sky overhead.

After four hours of bumps and jumps on the trails we decided to call it a day. Chad was unusually quiet on our ride home. A few groans interrupted the silence as my husband began to describe, in detail, how much every muscle ached. He could hardly wait to get home to take a hot shower and grab the heating pad. I suddenly remembered I packed a bottle of pain reliever – just in case. I popped off the top and offered him two pills. He could hardly contain his relief and I was glad I had something to make him feel better. It wasn't a million dollars, but at that moment, it was a gift that was quite comparable!

> "IF YOU SINFUL PEOPLE KNOW HOW TO GIVE GOOD GIFTS TO YOUR CHILDREN, HOW MUCH MORE WILL YOUR HEAVENLY FATHER GIVE GOOD GIFTS TO THOSE WHO ASK HIM."
> —MATTHEW 7:11

Matthew 7 says that if we as humans know how to give good gifts how much more does our heavenly Father give wonderful gifts to those who ask Him. Through His Word,

God also offers a gift that brings healing. Whether it is relief from physical or emotional pain, God's truth provides a remedy. He is our Healer, but it is up to us to accept His "medicine" or not.

Choosing to take His medicine involves placing our trust in Him and following His instruction. When we listen and heed God's direction written in Scripture, we can be confident we are taking the proper prescription that will eventually alleviate our pain. This healing we receive from God truly is… a wonderful gift.

SORT IT OUT

- Is there certain pain in your life that needs to be healed?
- Ask God to show you the first step to begin the healing process.
- Praise Him for His healing power.

ALL MIXED UP

After thirteen years of marriage the hand-held mixer I received as a wedding gift finally conked out. I could not afford the one I really wanted, the deluxe free-standing model with all the fancy attachments, so my mother-in-law gave me her aunt's 30-year-old antiquated mixer. Aunt Ceola spent most of her time in the kitchen so I was sure this mixer had seen its better day. But I was in a pinch, so this would have to do.

In the middle of my Christmas baking, I was secretly bemoaning the fact that I had to use this old thing. I thought to myself, "If only I had one of those new mixers that matched my kitchen everything I made would taste better. Baking would be less time-consuming and a whole lot easier." God gently impressed some thoughts upon my heart and from the back of my mind came a soft whisper, "This is what Aunt Ceola used and everything tasted great. The difference isn't the mixer but in who is using it."

> "NOW GLORY BE TO GOD! BY HIS MIGHTY POWER AT WORK WITHIN US, HE IS ABLE TO ACCOMPLISH INFINITELY MORE THAN WE WOULD EVER DARE TO ASK OR HOPE."
> —EPHESIANS 3:20

I was humbled and reminded that sometimes I am like that mixer. By myself I am just a standard model, nothing fancy, yet able to do the job. But if I allow the Holy Spirit to control me, I am capable of doing so much more than I could ever imagine. I paused and confessed my attitude to the Lord, then went back to stirring my cookie batter with a new, less "mixed up" perspective.

SORT IT OUT

- Could your attitude be holding back something exciting God has planned for you?

- Confess any negativity to God and ask Him to refresh you with His Spirit.

- Be open to God's leading…He has your best interest at heart!

ANNOUNCEMENTS

Is your mailbox flooded daily with junk mail like mine?

Every day I receive anything from credit card applications, flyers, of course, bills and unwanted solicitations. It amazes me how some companies get my address and assume I am the slightest bit interested in their offers.

As I flip through the envelopes, there is always one that catches my eye. It is a card with my name and address handwritten. That is my clue this is something personal.

I enjoy receiving cards and notes, but I especially enjoy birth announcements. There are so many cute cards with adorable designs! One of my favorites was a picture of a newborn wrapped in a pink bow with a tag that read, "Gift from God." The arrival of a new baby certainly stirs warm emotions in us and after receiving the good news I can't wait to go bring a gift to the new baby.

> "SUDDENLY, AN ANGEL OF THE LORD APPEARED AMONG THEM... 'THE SAVIOR-YES, THE MESSIAH, THE LORD – HAS BEEN BORN TONIGHT IN BETHLEHEM, THE CITY OF DAVID!'"
> —LUKE 2:9A, 11

I cannot imagine being one of the shepherds who, over 2,000 years ago, received the greatest birth announcement ever! An angel, joined by a vast host of others, proclaimed Jesus' birth. How exciting! The shepherds did the same thing we do; they visited the baby and then told everyone what had happened. The Bible does not tell us if they brought a gift. I'm sure there wasn't a Gymboree or Baby Gap on the corner in Bethlehem. But what they brought was much more important than a new outfit or soft blanket – they brought their hearts.

Their action shows what God desires from us the most. He doesn't care about money or possessions; what He longs for is our heart. A heart that believes and obeys Him is a wonderful way to announce His birth!

SORT IT OUT

- What is the condition of your heart today?
- Are you committed to God and experiencing a personal relationship with Him? Why not solidify or renew your commitment to Him now.

ANSWERED PRAYER

My seven-year-old son, Cameron, lost his glasses. I looked high and low; I practically tore the house apart! I felt like the widow in the Bible who searched all over for her lost coin. I looked under beds, in closets, dresser drawers, toy baskets, junk drawers – everywhere! In each "search and rescue" attempt, I rattled off a prayer asking the Lord to show me where Cam's glasses were.

As the days wore on my prayers were getting more desperate. I would pray, " Lord, please, I know you know where they are; will you please show me?" The next day my prayer would be, "Lord, he really needs them, don't you care about his poor little eyes?" Exhausted from the exercise of going from my tiptoes to all fours, I finally cried out, "Lord, what is it going to take? What is the point I am missing here? Please show me where they are!"

"ANYTHING IS POSSIBLE IF A PERSON BELIEVES."
—MARK 9:23B

A few days later as I was putting dishes away, still pleading with God, Cameron walked into the kitchen. He looked determined – a boy on a mission – so I asked him what he was doing. "Looking for my glasses," he told me. I pulled out a chair from the table and said, "Cam, why don't we just sit down and pray. Let's ask God to show us where your glasses are. He knows everything. He can help us find them."

I hoped my words sounded more confident than my heart felt. Cameron agreed and even little sister Madison folded her hands as we asked for God's help. After saying "amen" I whispered in my heart, "Lord, don't let him down. He believes in you."

Cameron got up from the kitchen table and headed toward the living room. I called out, "I already looked in there!" But he walked over to the desk, got down on his hands and knees and reached under the chair. There in the dark were his glasses!

He smiled as he put them on his face. I was speechless. I sat there trying to process what just happened and recalled the last few words I said to the Lord which were, "What is it going to take…he believes in you." In a soft voice came a reply, "All it takes is a simple act of faith in the heart of my child. He believes; why don't you?"

SORT IT OUT

- Have you been on your knees continually, waiting for God to answer your prayer? Keep praying and believing!

- Ask the Lord to increase your faith.

BUT THE SIGN SAYS!

Like most women, I love to shop. Although, I prefer to shop with my girlfriends rather than my husband. Women have a natural understanding of "shopping etiquette." For example, one rule is you don't buy something in the first store. You must exhaust all possibilities and, if what you were looking for was in the first store, then go back. Men tend to think if you like it in the first store, buy it and go home – mission accomplished.

One particular outing I happened to be with my husband, Chad. We were looking for a new jacket. The big sign on the easel outside the storefront said, "All Leather Coats and Outerwear 50% off." We entered the store, looked around and found one we liked that had some leather trim. The coat was hanging on the rack with other like jackets and had a sign above that read, "SALE - 50% off." We looked at the tag and liked the price, so we took it to the register.

> "DEAR FRIENDS, IF OUR CONSCIENCE IS CLEAR, WE CAN COME TO GOD WITH BOLD CONFIDENCE. AND WE WILL RECEIVE WHATEVER WE REQUEST BECAUSE WE OBEY HIM AND DO THE THINGS THAT PLEASE HIM."
> —1 JOHN 3:21-22

The sales clerk rang up the coat and gave us the total - the total without subtracting the discount. My husband began to question. He told her he was under the impression that ALL coats were 50 percent off. She replied, "I'm sorry, this one isn't on sale." Chad quickly responded, "Then why does the sign above the rack say fifty percent off?" They went back and forth for a few minutes until finally Chad walked to the front of the store, grabbed the sign and hauled this huge piece of poster board back to the register. (By this time I was halfway down the corridor in search of the nearest plant to hide behind!)

"Your sign says ALL leather coats and outerwear – fifty percent off!" His tone implied, "What part of this don't you understand?" The manager overheard the conversation, walked over to the register and said in a huff, "Just give him the discount for crying out loud!"

The clerk rang up the sale and Chad walked out proudly carrying his new jacket. He found me in a plastic fichus tree with my face as red as the sale sign. I assured him he had a point; I just didn't want to stick around to hear how he was going to prove it. He just kept repeating…"But the sign said!"

During my prayer time with God my thoughts flashed back to that shopping trip. I regained my focus and continued praying, asking God to help me overcome selfishness that held a stronghold in my heart. But at the same time, I felt Satan hissing messages of doubt and fear. The Holy Spirit assured me "[I] can be confident that He will listen to [me] whenever I ask Him for anything in line with His will" (1 John 5:14).

I know that overcoming selfishness is aligning with God's will. God wants me to live in victory. His sign, the Bible, tells me so! My spirit rose in confidence as I resisted Satan's schemes. I told him, "Get out of here, Satan, you can't mess with me – just read the sign!"

SORT IT OUT

- Do you often hear Satan hiss words of doubt and fear?

- Ask God to strengthen your mind so you can resist the devil. Praise Him because His Word is true and powerful!

CARRY ME

I turned around on the staircase and heard a little voice say, "Mommy, carry me!" I swooped up two-year-old Madison and plopped her on my hip where she has been perched many times. She fits perfectly there and she knows it. Whenever my little girl gets tired or sheds a tear, that's where she inevitably ends up. I offer soothing words of comfort and snuggle into her neck, kiss her soft skin or smell her light brown hair. I enjoy her here just as much as she does; it's a comfort thing, I guess. Today the dryer buzzer interrupted our moment so I set her down and off she went to play.

God comforts me much in the same way. Every time I get tired or hurt I cry out, "Jesus, carry me!" And He does. My soul is soothed when I feel Him pick me up and put me on His hip. He comforts me with His promises that assure me He knows what I'm going through. After all, He's carried me before. He carried me to the cross and overcame everything that gives me those bumps.

> "PRAISE THE LORD; PRAISE GOD OUR SAVIOR! FOR EACH DAY HE CARRIES US IN HIS ARMS."
> —PSALM 68:19

Satan tries to ruin our fellowship by placing doubts in my thoughts and feeding my mind with lies, "He doesn't really know how you feel; he's just full of empty promises."

Sometimes I feel myself slip, but something always jerks me back. The Holy Spirit alerts me to the truth of God's Word – just like the dryer buzzer! Whenever I am discouraged or hurt all I have to do is reach up. I believe God is there and I'm so thankful He never gets tired of carrying me.

SORT IT OUT

- Has life dealt you some bumps and made you shed a few tears? Are you too tired to walk? Allow God to carry you today.

CLOSE BY

I take my son, Cameron, to karate class at our local elementary school. The session only lasts for 45 minutes so instead of dropping their kids off, most parents just wait in the hall. The adults are not allowed in the gym; we might become a distraction, so I pass the time by reading a book. My son was a little nervous the first few times, but I reassured him I would be close by-waiting right outside the door.

However, one week I needed to pick up my daughter, Carley, from volleyball practice across town. Pulling into the parking lot I explained to my little white belt that I would be right back, but he hesitated when I opened the van door. I asked him if he felt sick since he usually jumps right out. After a few more probing questions, I came to the conclusion he was afraid I was just going to leave him. I explained that the situation would be no different to him since he can't see me during class anyway. "But Mom," he replied, "at least I know you're out there in case I need you."

"THE LORD REPLIED, 'MY PRESENCE WILL GO WITH YOU, AND I WILL GIVE YOU REST."
—EX. 33:14 NIV

I agree with author, Lotte Bailyn, when she says, "Instant availability without continuous presence is probably the best role a mother can play." Little did I know how much it meant to Cameron that I was right outside the door. My presence alone gave him the confidence and reassurance that he was safe in karate class and all was well in his world.

Little boys aren't the only ones who need reassurance. I get nervous and afraid in my world, too, and I long to feel the presence of my heavenly Father. Just to know He is right beside me calms my fears and settles my heart.

No matter where I am God is always with me. If I dwell by the farthest ocean or climb the highest mountain, God is there. This truth gives me confidence to know when I am in the "karate classes" of life I can take a deep breath and press on because I know God is ever present and always close by.

SORT IT OUT

- Take a few moments to quiet your heart.
- Linger on the truth that God is right next to you and understands your heart.
- Praise Him for His unfailing love and presence.

CONVERSATIONS IN THE WATER

Something about water enhances my communication with God. I don't know why; maybe it is because He created it and walked on it! Whatever the reason, I seem to have my best conversations with Him in the shower or bathtub.

Today I was especially feeling down and upset. My body was soaking, yet my heart was splashing around. "I can't do this; I'll never get it. I'm just not good enough!"

God replied, "It's not about being 'good enough'; I just ask you to be faithful."

"But I can't!" my soul shouted back. "Don't you see," I argued, "I say hurtful things to the people I love, I'm not always a good example for my children, and I feel like I cause my husband so much stress!"

The Holy Spirit responded, "Let your light so shine before men, that they may see your good works and glorify your Father in heaven" (Matthew 5:16 New King James Version).

I shot back, "I can't! I'm cracked!"

"Good," my Father said. "That's all the more ways for my light to shine out. All those cracks and broken areas really allow my power to shine bright. If you were a whole, unbroken vessel how would others see me in you?"

"Oh." My soul started settling down.

"THE VOICE OF THE LORD IS OVER THE WATERS; THE GOD OF GLORY THUNDERS, THE LORD THUNDERS OVER THE MIGHTY WATERS."
—PS. 29:3 NIV

"You can still use me? I'm still in the game?"
"Yes."
"But it sounds so crazy! Who wants to listen to a broken, cracked pot?"

A Scripture verse played in my mind, "Trust in the Lord with all your heart, and lean not on your own understanding; in all your ways acknowledge Him and He shall direct your paths" (Proverbs. 3:5-6 NKJV).

As our conversation ended, I wish I could say all my worries swirled down the drain along with the soap bubbles. But as I grabbed the towel and dried myself off, our conversation did leave me feeling a bit cleaner on both the inside and out.

SORT IT OUT

- Is there frustration bubbling in your heart?

- Talk to God about it and ask Him to settle your spirit.

GIVE ME STRENGTH!

Remember the song that goes, "Mama said they'll be days like this?" My day began as "one of those days" this morning. It started right from the get-go since I woke up fifteen minutes late. My two year old, Madison, usually sleeps until I get my older boys on the bus; but today she decided to wake up while I was trying to motivate my youngest son, Cameron, to brush his teeth and find his glasses.

I stumbled down the stairs and sat Madison on the counter while I scrounged in the cupboard for something to throw in lunch boxes. With my back to her, I suddenly heard a crash and turned to find a dish shattered all over the kitchen floor. I swept up the shards of glass and listened to groans of "why can't we have waffles today?" I poured myself a cup of coffee and accidentally spilled some on my hand, which only added to my misery. And as I ran my fingers under cold water I witnessed Madison dump cereal all over the floor.

> "THE LORD IS MY ROCK, MY FORTRESS AND MY SAVIOR; MY GOD IS MY ROCK, IN WHOM I FIND PROTECTION. HE IS MY SHIELD, THE STRENGTH OF MY SALVATION, AND MY STRONGHOLD."
> —PSALM 18:2

By this time Cameron was trying to get his snow pants zipped and was missing one mitten. The clock was ticking and the bus was rounding the corner. I grabbed the mitten from under the chair, zipped up the snow pants, escorted Cameron to the door and kissed him goodbye in a less than affectionate manner. I closed the door with a sigh and headed straight for the last piece of chocolate cake! I thought to myself, "I don't care that it's not even eight o'clock!"

Suddenly an article I read yesterday filled my thoughts. The author stated, "Your strength will run out, but God's never will." How appropriate for me today! Instead of filling up on empty calories from chocolate cake I grabbed my coffee and Bible and nestled into the couch. I turned to Philippians 4:13, "I can do all things through Christ who strengthens me" (NKJV).

I reflected on the forty-five minutes that had just transpired and began to pray. Slowly my attitude started to change. I began to thank God for the food I had to feed my children, mittens to keep little hands warm and that no one was hurt by broken glass. As I closed my Bible I knew God's strength would help me get through the day…and maybe even help me resist that last piece of chocolate cake!

SORT IT OUT

- Do you ever have "one of those days?"

- Thank God for not just wanting to give you strength, but be your strength!

- Ask Him to strengthen you with an encouraging word of truth.

GOD'S JOURNAL

I turned on the shower and put my hand under the running water. I waited a few seconds for it to warm up before I stepped over the side of the tub. This is starting to become a ritual – me standing under the running water as tears stream down my face. When I feel my soul is emptied I grab the towel and dry off. This is my own private sanctuary – my secret. I'm not really hiding, but I don't have to give an account to anyone while my tears spill down the drain. I pour out my sorrows behind the shower curtain and I know the only one who hears my cries is God.

I also relieve my soul and process varied emotions through journaling. I write what I've learned in my quiet times with God and describe in detail how I'm feeling. One page can be filled with uplifting Scripture and the next entry is a rambling of dark prose.

> "THIS IS WHAT THE LORD, THE GOD OF YOUR ANCESTOR DAVID, SAYS: 'I HAVE HEARD YOUR PRAYER AND SEEN YOUR TEARS. I WILL HEAL YOU...'"
> —2 KINGS 20:5

God is the only One who truly understands me – I don't even understand me! My thoughts about myself are not the same as what God thinks. King David says He thinks "precious" thoughts about me. So I ask myself this question, "If God kept a journal, what would He write?"

Would my Creator fill the blank page with frustration?

Would He write poems? Maybe scribble my name and put a heart around it? He does know everything about me. He even keeps better records than I do because Psalm 139:16 says *each day* is recorded in His Book!

When I get to heaven I would like to read that book. I'm sure God would have a different perspective. And those tears... "You keep track of all my sorrows; you have collected all my tears in your bottle" (Psalm 56:8). I imagine those tear-filled bottles lined up and I will graciously take them down and pour my tears over His feet. We will remember them no more. I will sing to God a song of praise for "He will remove all of [my] sorrows, and there will be no more death or sorrow or crying or pain" (Revelation 21:4a).

The death of Jesus tore the curtain and allows us access to our Holy God. God's Son holds the power to heal our hearts and dry our eyes. In His sovereignty God knows what's best and how much we can handle. He sees us and cares about the agony of our soul. If only I can remember that next time I'm sniffling behind my own curtain.

SORT IT OUT

- Do you have a private sanctuary where you pour out your heart to God?

- May you be reminded today that God knows and cares about the anguish in your soul.

- Take a few moments to let that truth sink deep in your spirit.

I NEED A CHANGE

My driver's license expired which meant I had to get a new card and have my picture taken. I made sure I had lipstick on and ran my fingers through my hair. I stood in front of the camera and flashed a grin. I knew my picture wasn't going to be on the cover of a magazine but everyone from the grocery store clerk to the bank teller would look at that picture for another four years.

I didn't give it another thought until my updated license arrived in the mail. I compared my pictures as I took out the old card and replaced it with the new. Nothing really changed. My smile was the same and so was my hairstyle. Four years with the same style —I didn't think it had been that long!

Every six weeks I sit in the salon and flip through magazines searching for the perfect style. I want something new - hoping that it will lift my mood and give me a nice change. But every six weeks I walk out with the same, yet shorter, style that I had when I walked in.

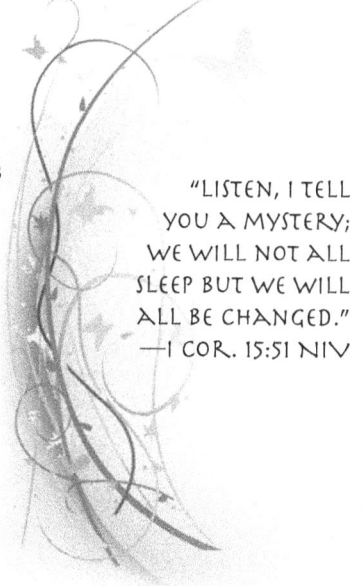

"LISTEN, I TELL YOU A MYSTERY; WE WILL NOT ALL SLEEP BUT WE WILL ALL BE CHANGED."
—I COR. 15:51 NIV

As Christians, we sometimes find ourselves in a similar pattern. Every Sunday we walk into church looking for something new—a change. We listen to the sermon, nod in agreement and then leave. But by Wednesday we have succumbed to the same bad habit we struggled with the week before. Nothing ever really changes and the cycle continues until our next Sunday appointment rolls around. Some folks are just content with their "spiritual hairstyle."

To change bad habits we must first want to change. The next step is to commit our plan to God and ask for His help. God's strength will help us as we implement the necessary action into our lives. The requirements are not always easy. They demand perseverance, but the desired results are most often worth our efforts. Trust God, ask for wisdom and follow His instruction. He has the power to change from the inside out and that feels better than a new hairstyle ever could!

SORT IT OUT

- Ask God if there is something in your life He wants to change for the better – perhaps it's a behavior or attitude.

- Pray for wisdom as you take the next step.

I SLIPPED!

If your children are anything like mine they often do careless things. As parents, we don't always understand their behavior. For example, my kids like to walk anywhere but where they are supposed to. If we are in a parking lot they walk on the curb; if we are in the park they pick the cement railing. This summer we took a trip to Lake Michigan and my son Alex chose the rocks that were staggered between the pier and the water.

These huge boulders had gaps between them, which posed the question, "Do I jump or go back to safety by Mom and Dad?" Alex chose option number one and instead of landing with a firm footing, he slipped right into the water. My husband grabbed his hand and pulled him up. As his parents, we reassured him that even though it was a foolish choice, we still loved him and were ready to pick him back up.

> "I WAS SO FOOLISH AND IGNORANT—I MUST HAVE SEEMED LIKE A SENSELESS ANIMAL TO YOU. YET I STILL BELONG TO YOU; YOU ARE HOLDING MY RIGHT HAND. YOU WILL KEEP ON GUIDING ME WITH YOUR COUNSEL, LEADING ME TO A GLORIOUS DESTINY."
> —PSALM 73:22-24

I don't know why I am constantly surprised when my kids do foolish things because I do them too. I can lose my temper and end up saying things I don't mean. I become impatient and act in ways I later regret. King David accurately depicts our human behavior in Psalm 73 as he describes us as senseless animals!

The good news is that no matter how senseless or foolish my choices are, because I believe in Jesus' saving power, I will always belong to God. I have hope because I am His child! God is my Father who loves me, guides me and is continually leading me toward a glorious destiny! I am so thankful that my heavenly Father understands my behavior and will always pick me up after my foolish choices cause me to slip.

SORT IT OUT

- When we make foolish choices and slip God still holds our hand. It is easy to get discouraged when it happens over and over.

- Be encouraged! God never gets tired of picking us up, brushing us off and putting us back on the right track.

ICY REFLECTIONS

One Sunday morning as my family headed off to church, I stayed behind to get some last minute things organized for a special event after the service. It was a bitter, cold morning – the kind that takes your breath away. I went out in the garage to warm up my van and after several trips in and out, which resulted in frozen fingers, I asked God, "Why did you make it so unbearably cold today?"

Finally, after everything was ready, I climbed into my warm car. As I pulled out of my driveway, I felt like I was entering an enchanted world. Before me was a beautiful winter wonderland! Fresh snow had fallen the night before and left everything covered in glistening white. The most breathtaking picture was the sun sparkling through the trees as every branch was completely outlined in ice. I stared in awe as the limbs sparkled and twinkled and then realized the frigid temperature is what helped create this amazing scene.

> "SO WHEN WE ARE WEIGHED DOWN WITH TROUBLES, IT IS FOR YOUR BENEFIT AND SALVATION!"
> —2 COR. 1:6A

God's message whispered to me, "You had to endure the cold in order to enjoy the beauty." And so it is with life. Trials come into our lives and leave us with that unbearably cold, bitter feeling. But just about the time we think we won't ever thaw out is often when we begin to see the blessings God intended during our "cold spell."

We are better able to empathize with others who may have had a drop in temperature too. Second Corinthians explains when God comforts us, it is so we, in turn, can comfort others who are hurting. Whether it is a kind word, a prayer lifted on their behalf or a shared cup of coffee, we can be sure those simple acts of kindness can warm up even the coldest of hearts.

SORT IT OUT

"Lord, I know the trials you allow help make me more like you. Help me to remember that and use my experiences to help others. Amen."

IMPRINTS ON THE HEART

My pastor once told me that I am not the type of person who would look at the truth and then refuse to believe it. I do believe God's Word is absolute truth and it has the power to cut deep into our innermost thoughts. His truth has the ability to expose us for who we really are.

Since I firmly believe the Bible is true I also trust each person is uniquely created according to God's master design. I had no control over the color of my eyes, my height, if I would have freckles and curly hair or dark skin and straight hair.

The same truth applies to my children. My four kids have very different personalities, but when it comes to their looks, that is another story. My husband, Chad, has very prominent genes and our children look just like him. When people comment on how much our kids resemble Chad, I usually jokingly reply, "I must have blank DNA!"

But as crazy as it sounds —that's what I used to think! I secretly felt God decided I didn't have any redeeming qualities that were worth passing onto my children. I took this idea to heart and sometimes felt like the "outsider" inside my own family!

Going back to what my pastor said, I don't want to refuse

> "SO GOD CREATED MAN IN HIS OWN IMAGE, IN THE IMAGE OF GOD CREATED HE HIM; MALE AND FEMALE CREATED HE THEM. THEN GOD LOOKED OVER ALL THAT HE HAD MADE, AND HE SAW THAT IT WAS EXCELLENT IN EVERY WAY…"
> GENESIS 1:27-31 KJV

the truth. I began to examine my thought process and ask myself if my mind was playing tricks on me? Was Satan trying to persuade me to think negatively? Was my pride controlling me? All of those questions bounced around in my mind and the truth of what really matters became twisted.

I finally concluded that in twenty-five years it was not going to matter who my children looked like. I learned that just because my kids don't resemble me physically, they could mirror me spiritually. And as their mother, it is my job to pass on spiritual traits so my children are equipped to impact the world for God's glory. I'm thankful for the privilege to teach my children about God's character and imprint truth into their soul, which I believe, matters more to God than passing on button noses and birthmarks!

SORT IT OUT

- God made you wonderfully unique! What traits would you like to pass on that will make an eternal difference?

- Focus on one quality today.

IS THERE LIFE ON OTHER PLANETS?

My family and I took a road trip to an amusement park. Our adventure was packed full of thrills, shrills and walking – lots of walking! After a long day we located our car and welcomed the chance to finally sit down. It was my turn to drive since my husband took the early morning shift.

When we started out the sun was just beginning to set. I wound our van around back roads watching the sky fade from blue to orange then red and finally dark gray. My kids were settling into their little nests and my husband was tilted back getting some shut-eye. I popped one of my iPod earphones in and prepared to cruise the night away. I hoped the music would distract me from the heavier issues that were weighing on my mind. I quietly hummed and tried to push back those thoughts like branches interrupting a forest path.

> "HE SHAKES THE EARTH FROM ITS PLACE, AND ITS FOUNDATIONS TREMBLE. IF HE COMMANDS IT, THE SUN WON'T RISE AND THE STARS WON'T SHINE. HE ALONE HAS SPREAD OUT THE HEAVENS AND MARCHES ON THE WAVES OF THE SEA. HE MADE ALL THE STARS...HIS GREAT WORKS ARE TOO MARVELOUS TO UNDERSTAND...."
> —JOB 9:6-10

I drove along and noticed the sky had a lot of cloud cover - even the stars seemed to be hiding. All except one. Straight ahead was a bright light the size of a pinprick peeking through the dark curtain. It caught my attention and had me mesmerized for a few moments.

I remembered the brighter stars are actually planets and I imagined what it must look like up close.

I visualized the speck of light as if I were looking through a telescope. I'm sure it would appear completely different than what I imagine. My thoughts suddenly jarred as it felt like someone was tapping on my shoulder. The Holy Spirit whispered, "If you zoomed in on God you'd also see a different picture. Look closer and you'll find He is much bigger than the scope of your imagination."

I snapped to attention and sat upright in my seat. What? It became clear to me that I was trying to figure things out on my own. The Holy Spirit reminded me God is bigger than my circumstances and when I keep my eyes on Him, my problems seem so small.

Traffic started getting heavier and my attention turned back to the highway. When it finally cleared I looked up in the sky. My light was gone, as it had done its job for the night. I began to look at my circumstances differently and my heart settled as I remembered God has my situation under control.

Next time my kids ask if there is life on other planets I'm going to answer, "Yes" and that "Life" communicates with us too.

SORT IT OUT

"Lord, you are awesome and full of power. Your greatness is hard for me to understand. Thank you for the beauty of your creation and the gentle reminders you use to pull my thoughts toward you. Amen."

LAMP LOVER

I love lamps. I know that might sound a bit unusual. But I love the way their soft light creates a warm and cozy atmosphere. My husband doesn't share my appreciation so when he comes home he goes from room to room turning off their light. I'm a bit sad as he snuffs them out. I feel that while they sit they are just waiting for the next opportunity to do what they were meant to do – shine their little lights out! I suppose they do need a break now and then and if they were on all the time, I might not appreciate them the way I do.

I can identify with those little lamps. I do my best to shine brightly. I try to keep my house clean, exercise regularly and serve healthy food to my family. I try to keep up with the piles of laundry and I baby-sit for my neighbor when she needs a break. But sometimes the more I try, the dimmer my lamp becomes!

Finally, I get to the point of desperation where I just need a break. I need to stop, look and listen. Stop running around. Look at what is priority and listen for God's direction. As I take a deep breath, I ask myself, "What am I supposed to do now?" I have to make a choice.

Jesus says, "Are you tired? Worn out? Come to me. Get away with me and you'll recover your life. I'll show you

> "YOU ARE TO LIVE CLEAN, INNOCENT LIVES AS CHILDREN OF GOD IN A DARK WORLD FULL OF CROOKED AND PERVERSE PEOPLE. LET YOUR LIVES SHINE BRIGHTLY BEFORE THEM."
> —PHIL. 2:15

how to take a real rest. Walk with me and work with me – watch how I do it. Learn the unforced rhythms of grace...." (Matthew 11:28-29 The Message).

After soaking in those words of refreshment, my heart becomes renewed and energized. I'm able to get back on track - ready to go out and shine brighter in my own little world.

SORT IT OUT

- Perhaps you need a break. Take some time for yourself and ask God for wisdom as you evaluate your priorities today.

LET'S GET MOVING

My husband and I have moved four times in the last sixteen years so I know how stressful the entire process can be. The wrapping, packing and organizing of boxes can become overwhelming. So when I read about the men in the Bible God directed to move, I can certainly identify. I know they didn't have U-Haul trucks to make it any easier, and I'm sure they, too, felt overwhelmed.

Abraham comes to mind first. God called him from his father's land and prompted him to go to a distant place while making great promises. Moses traveled with the Israelites for 40 years, never staying put for very long. The New Testament tells of Paul who went from land to sea to jail only to do it all over again several times!

God's purpose is no different today. He calls each one of us to Him and longs for us to know Him, believe Him and obey Him. Each of us has different circumstances, but nevertheless, God's desire is still the same.

> "BUT NONE OF THESE THINGS MOVE ME, NEITHER COUNT I MY LIFE DEAR UNTO MYSELF, SO THAT I MIGHT FINISH MY COURSE WITH JOY, AND THE MINISTRY, WHICH I HAVE RECEIVED OF THE LORD JESUS, TO TESTIFY THE GOSPEL OF THE GRACE OF GOD."
> —ACTS 20:24 KJV

We really have several choices when God calls us to action. We can choose to ignore the prompting by turning 180 degrees the other way. We can rationalize our situation by getting out a legal pad and writing "pros vs. cons." Or we can act in faith and move with God, trusting Him to guide our steps.

I was facing a situation where God was calling me to move. My thoughts swished in my mind like clothes in a washing machine. I was wrestling with my choices and having a hard time making a decision. I tried to distract myself and began painting.

I covered the grass in my backyard with a drop cloth and began. Partway through my task the wind started picking up and I noticed dark clouds looming to the west. I painted a little faster and kept a close watch on the obscure masses lumbering in. When finished, I lay on my back and contemplated my situation as I soaked up the last remaining sunbeams peeking through the dark curtain above.

Moments later I opened my eyes only to notice there were two layers of clouds. The wind was blowing and my eyes could barely keep up with their pace. I concentrated on the first layer as it looked like God's fingertips were pushing them along.

The first drop of rain hit my shoulder just as God whispered to me, "I'm still in the business of moving things. I can do clouds, but I prefer people." A peace settled in my soul as I handed my situation over to Him. I grabbed my brush and headed to the house. "Okay, God," I said, "Here is my heart…I'm ready to get moving."

SORT IT OUT

"Lord, it's hard sometimes to do the right thing. It is a struggle that never seems to go away. Help me make good decisions. Move in my heart and help me to obey you. Amen."

LET'S TALK

The old saying that goes, "There are three forms of communication: telephone, telecom and telewoman" brings a chuckle to some women and offends others.

Of course, this depends what kind of woman she is. Yes, the studies show that girls are more verbal than boys - that's just how God made us. The question is, "What do we talk about?" Everything! It doesn't matter if it's our baby's diaper rash, a trip to the grocery store or a pile of laundry - we can always find something to say.

With that capability comes responsibility. Too much of a good thing is not always good. Solomon wrote that "even fools are thought to be wise when they keep silent; when they keep their mouths shut, they seem intelligent" (Proverbs 17:28).

I don't want to "seem" intelligent – I want to be intelligent! It appears the choice is mine. I am the only one who controls what comes out of my mouth and, unfortunately, I am capable of saying anything! One minute a passage of Scripture rolls off my tongue and in the next breath I fling a snippy remark at my husband.

> "DON'T TALK TOO MUCH, FOR IT FOSTERS SIN. BE SENSIBLE AND TURN OFF THE FLOW!"
> —PROVERBS 10:19

My prayer is that the Holy Spirit helps me control my tongue as the psalmist writes, "You have tested my thoughts and examined my heart in the night. You have scrutinized me and found nothing amiss, for I am determined not to sin in what I say" (Psalm 17:3). My heart's desire is to say things that only please God. How about you? What are your heart's desires? Want to talk about it?

SORT IT OUT

- What do you like to talk about? Words have tremendous power to help or hurt.

- Ask God to help you think before you speak.

MACK THE DOG

We have a rule in our neighborhood that all dogs must be on a leash. Occasionally, our Scottish terrier, Mack, spots a squirrel across the road and if one of my kids leaves a crack in the door, Mack views this as his open invitation to the great outdoors! Usually the only way to call him home is to get in the van and pretend to go "bye bye." He spots our van and comes "a' runnin.'"

One day as this scenario unfolded, I decided to actually take Mack on some errands with me. He hopped up in the front seat and enjoyed his tour of our small town. After being gone for several hours, I pulled into the garage and opened his door. I assumed Mack would be glad to be home, but instead of jumping down and running into the house, he just sat and stared at me. I thought to myself, "You dumb dog! Why would you want to stay out here in this cold, dark garage when you are invited into a home that is complete with food, water and a warm fire to boot?"

> "I PRAY THAT THE EYES OF YOUR HEART MAY BE ENLIGHTENED, SO THAT YOU WILL KNOW WHAT IS THE HOPE OF HIS CALLING, WHAT ARE THE RICHES OF THE GLORY OF HIS INHERITANCE IN THE SAINTS, AND WHAT IS THE SURPASSING GREATNESS OF HIS POWER TOWARD US WHO BELIEVE."
> —EPH. 1:18-19A NASB

Every so often I am reminded that I can be that "dumb dog!" How many times do I turn down rich spiritual invitations? I give up the comfort of peace when I decide to stay up all night mulling over my problems. I miss God's blessing when I'm stingy and withhold good from those in need. I give up being filled with joy because I'm too busy looking at the glass half empty.

It took some coaxing, but like the prodigal son, Mack returned to his favorite spot in front of the fire. I hope the next time I'm drawn to sit in the cold, dark garage God's Spirit will remind me of what I'm giving up – a peaceful place by the fire next to my heavenly Father.

SORT IT OUT

- God's abundant riches are for our benefit!
- Ask God to show you if a particular habit keeps you from experiencing God's blessing.

MITTEN ACCOMPLISHED

There are fine lines a woman must walk after she becomes a mother. So many emotions and feelings are intricately woven into the fabric of motherhood. The responsibility of caring for a child is simply delightful, yet at times can be terribly heartbreaking.

Mothers must make split second decisions and rely on gut instincts. Being fair is one of the more difficult aspects of the role. As her two children stare expectantly into her eyes, a mother must decide who had the toy first. She must successfully divide the cookie into equal pieces to avoid any possibility of a meltdown. She must keep a mental checklist to remain in good standing as an "equal opportunities" parent.

Discipline is another aspect where mothers use wisdom gleaned from past experiences. We constantly ask ourselves the questions, "How long should the "time out" be? What privilege should be taken away this time?"

> "SING TO THE LORD, ALL YOU GODLY ONES! PRAISE HIS HOLY NAME. HIS ANGER LASTS FOR A MOMENT, BUT HIS FAVOR LASTS A LIFETIME! WEEPING MAY GO ON ALL NIGHT, BUT JOY COMES WITH THE MORNING."
> —PSALM 30:4-5

I wrestled with these questions the winter my son had difficulty keeping track of his mittens. Early in the season we had a plethora in all shapes and sizes. As winter progressed, our bounty dwindled as my son lost every pair.

My emotions swished through my mind like a load of laundry. I wavered between teaching him a lesson to running out and buying a new pair. My gut told me to hold him accountable for his actions, but my heart refused to send him out with bare little hands. I went with my gut and watched him as he waited for the bus with uncovered, clenched fists.

A sneering voice in the back of my mind told me I was a cruel army commander sending him off to war without proper armor. I took a deep breath and silently assured myself I was doing the right thing – he had to learn the hard way.

However, as soon as his bus pulled away I jumped in my car and drove to each store in town. To no avail: none had any mittens left. I started to despair as I made the final stop. I walked in the door and saw an entire wall filled with mittens – my heart skipped a beat!

A few short hours later I watched my son walk up the driveway with his head down and hands buried deep into his coat pockets. I opened the door and presented him with the new mittens. He humbly accepted my gift and I could tell by the look on his face – "lesson learned."

Even as an adult, I sometimes lose my "mittens." Like my son's cold hands I tend to learn best through the uncomfortable circumstances God allows in my life. Those situations give me the opportunity to grow closer to God and after the lesson is learned, I feel God wrap His love around me. His renewed presence feels as warm and comforting as a new pair of mittens.

SORT IT OUT

- As you look back on your own life, can you see how God used some hard lessons for your benefit?

- Ask God to help you take the positive from those situations and use it to help others.

MY IMAGINARY FRIEND

When you were a child, did you have an imaginary friend? Maybe you didn't, but perhaps your own child does. Believe it or not, some moms have imaginary friends too! My "imaginary" friend shows up once in a while and all she likes to do is talk. She says things like, "Wow, you gave your toddler three Happy Meals this week?" "I can't believe you left your crawling baby in the room with scissors!" "You actually gave in to your two year old's temper tantrum?" "What kind of mother are you anyway?"

After listening to all this "talk" I start to wonder, "What kind of mother am I?" I begin to get discouraged and think, "Maybe I can't do this." That is just about the time my real friend steps in and says, "You know what, being a mom is hard work but I'm always here to help."

> "I NO LONGER CALL YOU SERVANTS... INSTEAD, I HAVE CALLED YOU FRIENDS."
> —JOHN 15:15 NIV

Thankfully, I really do have such a friend and He is not imaginary. My real friend, Jesus, does not judge, but encourages, listens and loves me no matter what I may be feeling at the moment. Without His constant help, motherhood would be harder than it already is! That seems impossible since there are days I wonder if I'm going to make it until naptime – much less bedtime!

The good news is that Jesus extends His friendship to anyone. He shows no favoritism and, unlike the criticism from my imaginary friend, Jesus says, "I know you can do this because I will guide you and be your strength. I know you are exhausted; just come to me and I will give you rest."

There is a huge difference between these two friends. One just messes with my imagination and the other far exceeds anything my imagination could ever hope for or dream of.

SORT IT OUT

- Which "friend" do you listen to most?
- Ask the Holy Spirit to help you discern the lies from the truth.

NEW THINGS

Vacuuming is not my favorite chore. But today there was something different about this very mundane task. We just laid new carpet and it was fresh, clean and smooth! I told my kids their lives might be in danger if they spilled on the new carpet. (They knew I wasn't too serious, but they sure got my point!) There is just something energizing about getting new things. The look – the smell…from clothes to carpet we are simply attracted to new things.

God is the Creator of "newness." Each day He brings new life and new mercies! Sometimes we can see when God makes something new; other times we don't have any idea at all. Yet Isaiah 43:19 assures us that He is doing a brand new thing right now - making a pathway through the wilderness for His people to be refreshed.

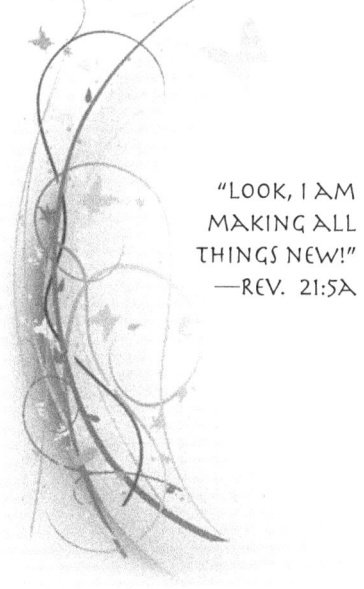

"LOOK, I AM MAKING ALL THINGS NEW!"
—REV. 21:5A

Sometimes life doesn't feel refreshing. It doesn't take much to make us feel beaten down to the point of despair. David expressed that feeling when he penned Psalm 40:1-3:

> "I waited patiently for the Lord to help me, and he turned and heard my cry. He lifted me out of the pit of despair, out of the mud and the mire. He set

my feet on solid ground and steadied me as I walked along. He has given me a new song to sing, a hymn of praise to our God."

David finishes with praising God for a new song! We might not see God's hand at work, but we can trust Him as David did. When our heart is discouraged, and we feel like we just can't go on, the Holy Spirit is able to breathe energy into us and give us a new song. This is just what we need to feel refreshed and renewed. Whether it's a new song or new carpet, we can always thank God for the new things He gives.

SORT IT OUT

- Has God done something new in your life?

- Do you have something new to be thankful for?

- Express your gratitude to God in your own unique way. Perhaps even sing a new song!

O B E Y

Objections, Bargains, Excuses, Yielding

Like many parents, my husband and I have asked our children to help out with the household chores. And like many children, I'm pretty sure my kids aren't the only ones to complain when told to carry out their responsibilities. My daughter Carley's job is to empty the dishwasher which she isn't always thrilled to do. She often tries to solicit help from her brother by asking, "Please, I'll pay you if you do it for me." When Alex is told to take out the trash, he most likely offers the excuse, "But, Mom, I'm in the middle of a playing my drums!" And when Cameron is reminded the dog dish is empty, he frequently objects, "That's not my job."

Our heavenly Father gives us responsibilities, too. His Word teaches us to love our neighbor, be kind, help others, and share the Good News. He also impresses on our hearts individual tasks that we, specifically, are designed to fulfill.

"BUT MOSES PLEADED WITH THE LORD, 'O LORD, I'M JUST NOT A GOOD SPEAKER. I NEVER HAVE BEEN, AND I'M NOT NOW, EVEN AFTER YOU HAVE SPOKEN TO ME. I'M CLUMSY WITH WORDS.'"
—EXODUS 4:10

God told Moses to go to Pharaoh and insist he free the Israelites from captivity, but Moses did not go without a fight! He pleaded with God – "Please, God, I'm not a good speaker. Lord, please, send someone else!" Usually when pleading begins, objections, bargaining and excuses are sure to follow. Like Moses and my children, none of us is exempt from this behavior.

Have you ever objected to God, "No, I just can't. What if it doesn't turn out like I plan?" Have you tried to bargain? "I will do it, but only if it works out this way." Or have you offered God excuses? "That's not really my personality."

God doesn't want objections, bargains or excuses – He wants a yielded spirit. God desires we humble ourselves and trust Him as we follow His instruction. God is pleased when we willingly cooperate with the prompting of His Spirit. To God—that is the best way to spell OBEY.

SORT IT OUT

"Lord, as the psalmist prays, 'Teach me…to follow every one of your principles. Give me understanding and I will obey your law…Make me walk along the path of your commands, for that is where my happiness is found.' Amen" (Psalm 119:33-35).

OFF KEY

Sunday is one of my favorite days of the week. I can't wait to go to church and hear our pastor present God's Word in his unique style and I also enjoy our worship time. I like to sit back, absorb the music and listen to fellow believers as they lift their voices in praise to God. Leading our worship is a group of very talented musicians whose voices are smooth, melodic – practically angelic!

One Sunday around Christmas I listened as the team sang, "Hark the Herald Angels Sing." I closed my eyes and envisioned the shepherds kneeling in awe as the multitude of angels sang the good news of Christ's birth. Even though I have probably sung this song a hundred times, it was hard not to get wrapped up in emotion.

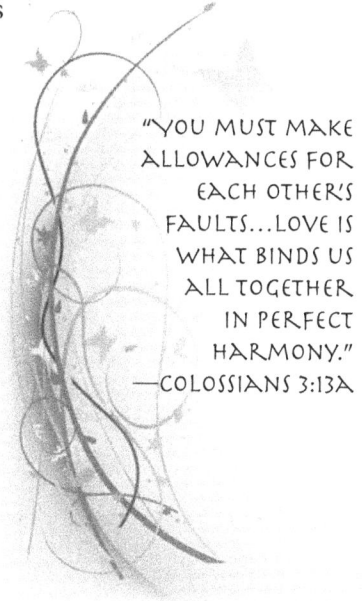

"YOU MUST MAKE ALLOWANCES FOR EACH OTHER'S FAULTS...LOVE IS WHAT BINDS US ALL TOGETHER IN PERFECT HARMONY."
—COLOSSIANS 3:13A

Suddenly, a screeching sound interrupted my soul from its worshipful state. I slowly opened my eyes and looked over at the person standing next to me. I silently cringed, as his voice - completely off-key - evoked the feeling of fingernails on a chalkboard. I felt a twinge of conviction, as it was clear this man was singing from his heart. I humbly asked God to forgive my judgmental attitude while being reminded of Colossians 3:12-14:

"Since God chose you to be the holy people whom he loves, you must clothe yourselves with tenderhearted mercy, kindness, humility, gentleness and patience. You must make allowance for each other's faults…and the most important piece of clothing you must wear is love. *Love is what binds us all together in perfect harmony*" (emphasis added).

I didn't need a sermon to be reminded that I have a few faults of my own and this time it was me who was "off key."

SORT IT OUT

"Lord, it's so easy to point out the flaws in others. Forgive me when I judge people. Help me to leave that job to you! Thank you for your forgiveness and grace. Amen."

ONE SHOT

On Sunday evenings I usually check my calendar and look ahead to the upcoming week. I make sure Carley's volleyball schedule is listed, my sons' basketball practices are scheduled and doctor appointments are penciled in. As I glanced over my calendar one week, I was reminded of a special event planned for the upcoming Saturday. I juggled a few appointments around in my planner and decided Thursday was the only day I could shop for an appropriate outfit.

Thursday arrived and, as usual, unexpected errands crept into my day that whittled away the allotted time. Instead of having the entire day free, I now had a window of about three hours. This was my only shot to find something dressy but not flashy, stylish and not frumpy!

> "LIVE WISELY AMONG THOSE WHO ARE NOT CHRISTIANS, AND MAKE THE MOST OF EVERY OPPORTUNITY."
> —COLOSSIANS 4:5

To a woman this is a serious mission, so I packed the diaper bag full of animal crackers, fruit snacks, books, toys and enough apple juice to water a camel. I was prepared to make this operation with my two year old in tow successful!

I made it to the mall and managed to find a few suitable things to try on. I grabbed the items off the rack and wheeled into a dressing room. Time was of the essence and so far, things were going according to plan.

My cell phone rang as I had one arm halfway through a silky shirt. I tucked the phone between my ear and shoulder and explained to my friend why I couldn't talk. I told her this was my one and only opportunity to shop for a special outfit. She completely understood and, as a woman, she sympathized with my plight.

I gathered my things and headed to the register thinking to myself that my life is like that, too. One chance is all I get! One shot to raise godly children, one shot to build a healthy marriage and one shot to impact my world for Christ. I know opportunities come and go, and some circumstances do allow for a second chance, but when it comes to truly living life – it's a one shot deal!

Next Sunday when I look at my calendar, I think I will try to schedule things a little differently.

SORT IT OUT

"Lord, teach me to number my days and make them count for eternity. Amen."

OPPOSITES ATTRACT

Do you remember back in elementary school when your science teacher explained that "opposites attract?" This concept goes beyond the realm of physics and also applies to relationships. My husband is very black and white where I tend to dwell in the gray area. He is very logical while I often dream. For the most part we get along great, but sometimes our differences create plenty of opposition instead of attraction!

Two women that Paul mentions in Philippians 4 were having a hard time getting along as well. Paul pleads with Euodia and Syntyche to stop fighting and settle their disagreement. They had worked hard alongside Paul in telling others the Good News. Perhaps they were such opposites and could not see eye to eye that it made their behavior unattractive.

There will always be people around who are hard to agree and get along with. It could be your spouse, parent, child, friend, co-worker or fellow Christ-follower that you struggle with and to save that relationship you must simply agree to disagree. But when it comes to sharing the Good News of salvation in Jesus let us heed the warning from Paul in 1 Corinthians 1:10:

> "THEN MAKE ME TRULY HAPPY BY AGREEING WHOLE-HEARTEDLY WITH EACH OTHER, LOVING ONE AN-OTHER, AND WORKING TOGETHER WITH ONE HEART AND PURPOSE."
> —PHILIPPIANS 2:2

> "Now, dear brothers and sisters, I appeal to you by the authority of the Lord Jesus Christ to stop arguing among yourselves. Let there be real harmony so there won't be divisions in the church. I plead with you to be of one mind, united in thought and purpose."

Let's pray that our differences don't cause others to oppose the gospel, but rather let us work together and show love, which can't help but attract them to Jesus.

SORT IT OUT

- Have you been struggling seeing someone through God's eyes?
- Ask God to show you some common ground to bridge the gap.
- Pray for God's love to flow through you to attract this person to Him.

MANIC MONDAY

I rolled over and looked at the clock on my night stand. The bright numbers read 7:15. I sighed and pulled the covers up to enjoy the remaining fifteen minutes before I had to be up and running. I usually look forward to Mondays – a quieter day that follows a busy weekend! My husband heads off to work and my older kids to school, so it's just me and Madi left at home. I wasn't as enthusiastic about today because as I lay there, I remembered the huge mess waiting to greet me as I started my day. Today had "Manic Monday" written all over it!

The fifteen minutes felt more like five as they quickly slipped by. I sat up and slid my feet across the carpet in search of my pink slippers. I grabbed my robe and plodded down the stairs. My boys were putting the finishing touches on their morning routine as I entered the kitchen. I signed homework papers and handed out lunch money; off they ran to catch the bus. I closed the door and surveyed the mess.

> "SO I DECIDED THERE IS NOTHING BETTER THAN TO ENJOY FOOD AND DRINK AND TO FIND SATISFACTION IN WORK. THEN I REALIZED THAT THIS PLEASURE IS FROM THE HAND OF GOD. FOR WHO CAN EAT OR ENJOY ANYTHING APART FROM HIM?"
> —ECCL. 2:24-25

Where do I begin? Dishes overflowed in the sink, cereal bowls littered the kitchen table, pillows were strewn across the living room floor and popcorn bowls sat on end tables. I swept from room to room gathering wet towels, dirty socks, making beds and hanging up clothes. I put Barbie back in her castle and Lego men returned to their space shuttle. As I sorted whites from darks, clouds started to roll over my spirit and I felt the doldrums settling in.

The morning passed quickly as the smell of Downy filled the house and I noticed it was already noon. Madi was getting hungry so I opened the cupboard and reached for the box of macaroni and cheese. I certainly worked hard all morning, but I felt like my efforts were in vain. I was a bit discouraged that my house would remain clean for only four more hours. Backpacks would soon line the foyer as shoes pile in front of the door.

I put the pan on the stove and set the timer for eight minutes. As I stared at the bubbling water, I felt my soul start to do the same. My morning felt very mundane and I started to compare my life to those of my friends. I glanced over at my refrigerator.

The Christmas card pictures taped to the front showed smiles that looked picture perfect. Cute kids gathered around sleds, fireplaces and brightly colored trees. Picture perfect families smiled under matching hats and mittens. I walked over to take a closer look.

I stared at each card individually and began to see something different – deeper. I realized they were people bonded together by joy and heartache. One family lost their mother, another struggled with a handicapped daughter, and a young couple was desperately praying for a child. My heart strayed from comparing myself to the illusion of perfection and, instead, began to identify with their joy and heartache.

Comparing yourself or your circumstances with someone else only gets you in trouble. Either depression sets in because you wish you had more or you become filled with pride because you think you are better off. My thoughts shifted back to the middle as I was reminded of how truly blessed I am.

Gaining a proper perspective can change things around.

I mixed the cheese into the noodles and prayed for my friends whose smiles graced my refrigerator. No, they are not perfect and neither am I. As my attitude changed, my spirit quickly went from the doldrums and hohums to praises lifted to the throne of grace. I thanked God for the blessings He gives and that my day turned out to be anything but a "Manic Monday."

SORT IT OUT

"Lord, I have so much to be thankful for. I know you have placed me here for a reason and have equipped me to do your work. Thank you for my hands that can serve you and help me keep my eyes on you – not others. Amen."

STANDING TALL

Stuck in traffic and lost in thought, I glanced around the landscape of our small downtown. Cars turned in front of me as the drivers hustled to reach their destination. Shoppers buzzed in and out of stores and leaves swirled around the sidewalk, warning me to hurry. My daughter's voice snapped back my thoughts like a twig over my knee as she said, "Mom, look at those men on top of that tall building!" I leaned over the passenger seat and craned my neck.

From my vantage point I saw two men walking around on top of the massive brick structure. I sat upright in my seat and said to my four-year-old, "Wow, that is something you don't see every day!" For a brief moment, time stopped as those of us who had our feet on the ground stared up in amazement. What we were seeing was definitely out of the ordinary.

For the most part, our days are made up of ordinary. But as Christ-followers, the power of the Holy Spirit gives us ample resource to go beyond ordinary. To be extraordinary means to "go out of the usual course and be exceptional."

In God's strength we are able to go out of our usual course and be exceptional when we show kindness, forgive

> "'YOU HAVE HEARD THAT THE LAW OF MOSES SAYS, 'LOVE YOUR NEIGHBOR AND HATE YOUR ENEMY.' BUT I SAY, LOVE YOUR ENEMIES! PRAY FOR THOSE WHO PERSECUTE YOU! IN THAT WAY, YOU WILL BE ACTING AS TRUE CHILDREN OF YOUR FATHER IN HEAVEN."
> —MATTHEW 5:43-44

others, and control our tongue. Jesus tells us that one of the best ways to be extraordinary, or above the crowd, is to love our enemies. This proves that we are His children. When the Holy Spirit powers our actions our lives soar above the ordinary. We might not walk on top of tall buildings, but we will sure be standing tall.

SORT IT OUT

"Lord, my spirit is willing, but my flesh is weak. I cannot love the way you want me to love without your power. Please help me, as I want to align my thoughts and actions in accordance to your Word so others can see you through me. Amen."

SWEET PERFUME

I have a weird habit; I am a "sniffer." I have a nose that knows! I smell everything from lotion and candles to new books and clean towels. Of course, I have my favorite scents – sheets fresh from the dryer and the smell of my baby when she wakes up from a nap. Some things have no fragrance, but there are also certain scents that really grab my attention like lilacs and caramel cappuccino.

The apostle Paul writes to the people of Corinth that "our lives are a fragrance presented by Christ to God. But this fragrance is perceived differently by those being saved and by those perishing. To those who are perishing we are a fearful smell of death and doom. But to those who are being saved we are a life-giving perfume" (2 Corinthians 2:15-16).

> "NOW WHEREVER WE GO HE USES US TO TELL OTHERS ABOUT THE LORD AND TO SPREAD THE GOOD NEWS LIKE A SWEET PERFUME."
> —2 COR. 2:14B

It is good to be reminded to care not only about how my laundry smells, but how my life "smells" to those around me. Do my actions have the aroma of sweet perfume or do I represent stench to everyone I come in contact with?

God commands us to "be imitators of God… and live a life of love, just as Christ loved us and gave himself up for us as a fragrant offering and sacrifice to God" (Ephesians 5:1-2 NIV). I know if my heart is right and my actions express God's love, my life can be a fragrant offering to Him – which is better than laundry or lilacs…to God, it's the sweetest smell of all!

SORT IT OUT

"Lord, I hope I "smell good" to those around me. I pray that my heart is clean and my actions encouraging! Use me to bless people today. Amen."

TEXT ME

My husband, Chad, recently bought a new cell phone for me with tons of cool features. My old cell phone served its purpose, but it doesn't even hold a candle to this new, thin, sleek one! My favorite tool is now "text messaging." I'm having a hard time scrolling through the letters so I am not very fast at typing a message. It takes me a few minutes to write one little sentence!

Since texting requires some time I need to keep my messages short and sweet. I found I can communicate with one word to make a point. I text "milk" if I need Chad to stop by the store and I punch in "call me" to reach Carley after school. I'm learning to narrow down my thoughts and just write the most important thing.

In my relationship with Jesus we communicate about different things too. Sometimes our conversations are long – like when I'm in the bathtub; other times they are just two- word little phrases, "Help me, save me, guide me." I also ask Him for patience with my children, wisdom in friendships and connection in my marriage. Jesus doesn't call back on my cell phone, but I hear His messages loud and clear.

> "AND NOW, O ISRAEL, WHAT DOES THE LORD YOUR GOD ASK OF YOU BUT TO FEAR THE LORD YOUR GOD, TO WALK IN ALL HIS WAYS, TO LOVE HIM, TO SERVE THE LORD YOUR GOD WITH ALL YOUR HEART AND WITH ALL YOUR SOUL, AND TO OBSERVE THE LORD'S COMMANDS..."
> —DEUT. 10:12-13

He impresses thoughts upon my heart – words He has written down in the Bible. Lately our conversations have the same theme. The underlying message I keep receiving is "love," no matter my situation. Jesus keeps reminding me love is patient, love the unlovely, love keeps no record of wrongs, love rejoices in the truth, love does not envy, love your neighbor, love your enemy, love always trusts, love never fails… on and on His message of love pours over me.

I understand for communication to be effective, you need to make your point clear and concise; and even then I need to hear a message often for it to sink in! So, yes, I think if God were to send me a text it would contain just one word– "love." And, hopefully, after receiving it a few times, I would eventually get the message!

SORT IT OUT

- What message God is sending you today?

- Is He asking you to forgive or help someone?

- Listen for His direction and ask Him to help you follow His instruction.

THAT'S NOT FAIR!

A common cry among siblings is, "That's not fair!" I often hear complaints such as "She has more than me"… "He sat in the front yesterday…" "I only have one and she has two"… "Why do I have to go to bed before him?" The list goes on and on. I try to keep things between my children as equal as possible, but it doesn't always work that way. Armed with motherly instinct, I attempt to intervene when I sense the mantra could chime at any moment. Although I must admit: I do fail, and at times it is inevitable I will hear the familiar cry, "That's not fair!"

I found myself saying the same words to my heavenly Father as I was reflecting over some life-changing events. "It's not fair, God! Why did you take my dad so soon? Why do I have this illness? Why was my father-in-law killed so tragically? It's just not fair!"

I paused and waited to see what God would say. Would He scold me and reply, "Whoever told you life was fair?" Or perhaps empathize with me and comfort my troubled heart.

> "AND I AM SURE THAT GOD, WHO BEGAN THE GOOD WORK WITHIN YOU, WILL CONTINUE HIS WORK UNTIL IT IS FINALLY FINISHED ON THAT DAY WHEN CHRIST JESUS COMES BACK AGAIN."
> —PHIL. 1:6

A picture unfolded in my mind and I saw myself sitting on a curb with my legs pulled tightly to my chest. I felt God scoot next to me and bow His head. He whispered words that were clear as a bell, "Tell me about it; it's not fair." He continued, "But unfortunately, that is how this sinful world works. I sure know how you feel, though."

"You do?"

"Remember my Son? It doesn't seem fair that He had to die for people who don't know Him or even care about Him – people who even curse Him. But I have a greater purpose. If you trust me, I can take your unfair moments and turn them into something good. After all, I did it with my own Son. So please be patient; my work is not yet finished. And sometimes the only way to accomplish my goal is in ways that seem 'not fair.'"

I nodded my head slightly and loosened the grip around my knees. I took a deep breath and sighed, "Okay, God, fair enough."

SORT IT OUT

"Lord, nothing in life is guaranteed – except your promises. Help me to trust you even when the path is dark, when I've been wronged and when things just don't seem fair! Help me keep an eternal perspective. Amen."

THE HUNGRY CATERPILLAR

On a sunny spring afternoon Madi crawled up next to me on our porch swing. She handed me one of our favorite books, *The Very Hungry Caterpillar*. I never grow tired of the story because each time I read it aloud, I learn something new. As the story goes the little caterpillar pops out of his egg and begins to search for food. On Monday he eats through one apple, but is still hungry. On Tuesday he eats two pears, but is still hungry. And on the story goes until Saturday when he eats through cake, ice cream, a pickle, Swiss cheese, salami, a lollipop, cherry pie, sausage, one cupcake and a slice of watermelon. Then the hungry little caterpillar gets a stomachache. The next day he eats a nice green leaf and feels much better.

> "I HAVE CHOSEN THE WAY OF TRUTH; I HAVE SET MY HEART ON YOUR LAWS."
> —PSALM 119:30 NIV

There on my porch swing I compared myself with the hungry little caterpillar. As my voice sing-songed over the pages, my mind was caught up in the Scripture I read earlier: "There is a way that seems right to a man, but in the end it leads to death" (Proverbs 14:12 NIV). Poor lil' caterpillar. He thought his way was right too!

And so it is with me. I rush through life trying to satisfy

my own appetites, thinking my way is right, but all I end up with is a spiritual stomachache! And just like the caterpillar who feels better after he eats what he is supposed to, I feel better when I take in God's Word. Jesus is called the Bread of Life and He satisfies better than a lollipop or slice of watermelon ever could!

SORT IT OUT

"Lord, I pray my desires are your desires. Satisfy my soul with your Word and make me a woman after your own heart. Amen."

TRUST ME

My girlfriends and I were sweating on the treadmills at our local gym, discussing the fact exercise was not our favorite thing. It takes a lot of discipline to be consistent in a fitness regimen and a lot of time before you see the results of your labor. We trudged along and I looked down at the machine, which said I had burned only 100 calories. I groaned, "Only 100 calories for all this hard work! That doesn't even cancel out one of the six cookies I ate yesterday!" It takes only thirty seconds to enjoy those cookies and a week of exercising to burn off the calories.

Trust is a lot like that. It takes a long time to build trust, but only a split second for it to become broken. No one in this world is perfect. We have all been hurt and disappointed by someone. Even King David cried out to God and lamented that his best friend, the one he trusted in completely – the one he even shared his food with – turned against him. Thankfully, the Holy Spirit comforts us in Psalm 9:10 by saying, "those who know your name trust in you, for you, O LORD, have never abandoned anyone who searches for you."

> "YOU WILL KEEP IN PERFECT PEACE ALL WHO TRUST IN YOU, WHOSE THOUGHTS ARE FIXED ON YOU! TRUST IN THE LORD ALWAYS, FOR THE LORD GOD IS THE ETERNAL ROCK."
> —ISAIAH 26:3-4

If you are placing your security and trust in your spouse,

your kids, your friends, your health or your money, be reminded that they will let you down. Turn to the Savior who never disappoints. God's promises are true – you can trust me on that!

SORT IT OUT

- Has someone hurt you so badly that you are having a hard time trusting again?

- Pour your heart out to God. Tell Him it's hard but you want to trust Him.

- Ask Him for wisdom today.

TUB TIME

A constant theme running through Scripture tells of God's mercy and unfailing love. Although He gets angry, He completely forgives even the "worst of sinners." A humble attitude and confession of sin calms His anger and restores our fellowship with Him. The other day I gained a deeper understanding of this truth while my little boy was taking a bath.

As I walked into the bathroom, it appeared Cameron thought he was in Lake Michigan by the way he was splashing around. Immediately, I was furious at the amount of water that had spilled onto the floor. Nonetheless, I grabbed a towel and spouted off the list of bath time rules through gritted teeth. By the tone of my voice he knew I was upset as he quickly hopped out of the tub. Cameron became overwhelmed with guilt and tears started to run down his already wet cheeks.

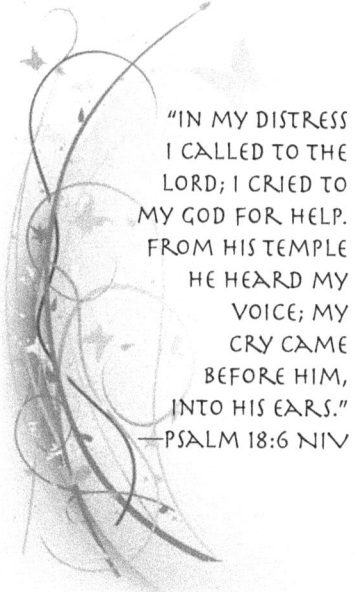

"IN MY DISTRESS I CALLED TO THE LORD; I CRIED TO MY GOD FOR HELP. FROM HIS TEMPLE HE HEARD MY VOICE; MY CRY CAME BEFORE HIM, INTO HIS EARS."
—PSALM 18:6 NIV

While standing on the bath mat shaking and shivering, he looked up and whispered, "Mommy, I'm sorry. Will you please help dry me off?" I took a deep breath and sent up a quick prayer asking God for strength. And as soon as I whispered, "Amen," my anger was gone and uncontrollable mercy flooded my heart. My compassion toward this dripping little boy became overpowering – all because he is the object of my love.

    I bent down and hugged his shaking shoulders. I spoke into his ear, "Of course, Cam. I love you no matter what – even when you splash water onto the floor!" God washed the truth over my soul that if I, in my human nature, can bestow small acts of mercy on those I love, how much more can my heavenly Father.

SORT IT OUT

- Praise God for His grace and mercy!
- Praise Him for His constant love!

THE FOURTH FLOOR

When I was in high school I had a summer job working in the office building where my dad was high on the corporate ladder. He was a well-respected boss in the accounting department and worked up on the fourth floor —where all the "important decisions" were made. I was just a 16-year-old girl who did the "dirty work" that no one else wanted.

One particular summer, my job consisted of constructing hundreds of flip charts by inserting index cards into plastic covers. It was a monotonous task that lasted all day…and took all summer long! It quickly became boring and tedious so when I needed a break I hopped on the elevator and rode up to the fourth floor.

When the doors opened, I would wind my way through the maze of cubicles to the corner office with the window. Even though I was pretty much the lowest employee in the building, people treated me differently because of who I was. I was introduced as "Jim's daughter - from the fourth floor." I liked the way that sounded as it made me feel important.

Whenever I knocked on his office door, my dad would

> "SO LET US COME BOLDLY TO THE THRONE OF OUR GRACIOUS GOD. THERE WE WILL RECEIVE HIS MERCY, AND WE WILL FIND GRACE TO HELP US WHEN WE NEED IT."
> —HEBREWS 4:16

immediately wrap up a conversation and I would be escorted to the chair by his desk. If someone else needed his attention he would politely say, "Give me just a minute" which sent the message I was top priority. I knew that my dad was busy, but sitting in his office made me feel special and loved. Not because of who I was, but whose I was.

As I was reading in Hebrews today my mind went back to those summer days and my trips up to the fourth floor. Paul's words reminded me that I have a heavenly Father who loves me more than I can even imagine. His "office" is always open and I can boldly go to Him with my honest heart. God says in Isaiah 43:4 that I am precious to Him, I am honored and He loves me…even more than I could ever experience sitting on the fourth floor.

SORT IT OUT

May you be reminded today that your heavenly father loves you way more than any earthly father ever could. Rest in His satisfying love today.

NO EXCUSE!

My daughter Madi and I were chitchatting in front of the bathroom mirror as I was brushing her hair. My husband entered, stood next to us and began to examine his own reflection. He was growing frustrated with his exercising efforts because they were not producing better results. He put his hands over his belly and declared, "Now, if I could just get rid of this, I'd be all set!" Without skipping a beat Madi piped up, "That's okay, Daddy, Mommy has that too!"

Seriously? My husband snickered and I wasn't sure if I should laugh or cry! I quickly regained composure and sing-songed a reply, "Well, Miss Madi, let me just say that Mommy has had four children so what's Daddy's excuse?"

I had to say something to get myself off the hook. Here I was frozen like a deer in the headlights – caught with my hand in the cookie jar! Yes, it's true, Mommy does have "that" too, but shouldn't I get even a little break? After all, having four kids does constitute lots of physical changes!

"FROM THE TIME THE WORLD WAS CREATED, PEOPLE HAVE SEEN THE EARTH AND SKY AND ALL THAT GOD MADE. THEY CAN CLEARLY SEE HIS INVISIBLE QUALITIES – HIS ETERNAL POWER AND DIVINE NATURE. SO THEY HAVE NO EXCUSE WHATSOEVER FOR NOT KNOWING GOD."
—ROMANS 1:20

I know, there is no such thing as a "good excuse," but I find myself making them all the time – especially to God. So many times I feel the Holy Spirit nudging me to do something good, but all I can muster up is a poor excuse.

Quite often my conversations with God go something like this:

"Why don't you invite them over for dinner?"
"But my house is a mess and laundry is piled everywhere!"

"Give her a call – she needs some encouragement."
"But I have so much to do today, I'll never get off the phone!"

"Your friend with the new baby could sure use a break."
"But if I take her older kids today she'll expect it all the time!"

Someone once said, "there will be no 'buts' in heaven for we will all be held accountable for our actions." Yes, I agree. That means I'd better get moving down here…after all, I really have no excuse!

SORT IT OUT

- Ask God to make you aware of poor excuses when they sneak up.

- Determine not to justify them and set your heart on doing right.

WINTER BOOTS

My family lives in Michigan, which means from November to March we spend most of our time putting on and taking off coats, hats, mittens and boots. With four children this can be a daunting task, especially during the winter I bought lace-up boots for my two small boys. (I must not have realized then that Velcro is a mother's best friend!)

One day after everyone was tired from making snow forts and tossing snowballs, my kids stumbled through the front door eager to start the process of undressing. My son Cameron dropped everything right where he was and began to take off his boots. He was cold and tired – anxious for some hot chocolate, but was having trouble with the laces. First he tried untying the frozen strings. When he found that did not work he started kicking the boots around as if they were going to magically fly off. The more he kicked the madder he became.

> "THEN IF MY PEOPLE WHO ARE CALLED BY MY NAME WILL HUMBLE THEMSELVES AND PRAY AND SEEK MY FACE AND TURN FROM THEIR WICKED WAYS, I WILL HEAR FROM HEAVEN AND WILL FORGIVE THEIR SINS AND HEAL THEIR LAND."
> —2 CHRON. 7:14

Finally, seeing his dilemma, I offered to give him a hand. His voice was quick and sharp, "No, Mom, I can do it." So I stepped back. It was hard for me to watch him struggle when I knew all I had to do was untie one little knot. Yet, he pressed on so I waited. I wondered how long he was going to persevere until he asked for help. After a few minutes, discouragement set in and he sheepishly accepted my offer. Within seconds the boots came off and my little boy was off enjoying that cup of hot chocolate.

My relationship with my own children reminds me of how I am still a child – God's child. When I have problems I often try everything in my power to fix them. I become filled with anxiety and I struggle, just like my son with his boots, as my heavenly Father just waits. He watches patiently, eager to help me, His child. But so often I am too proud and think I can do it "all by myself." I forget that God is much bigger than I am and when I ask for His help He gladly acts on my behalf. No problem is too big and God even cares about the little things – like taking off my boots.

SORT IT OUT

"Lord, forgive me for being too prideful to ask for your help. Please cultivate a humble heart in me – a heart that pleases you in all I do. Amen."

www.ingramcontent.com/pod-product-compliance
Lightning Source LLC
Chambersburg PA
CBHW051711040426
42446CB00008B/831